PLANTED IN GOD'S WORD

I0459140

DOMETRIA HALL

True Vine Publishing Co.

Planted in God's Word
Dometria Hall

Published by
True Vine Publishing Co.
810 Dominican Dr.
Nashville, TN 37228
www.TrueVinePublishing.org

Printed in the United States of America—First printing.

DEDICATION

This book is dedicated to the memory of Georgia Mae Moore, a faithful servant and true woman of God.

She lived each day deeply rooted in the Lord and His Word, leaving behind a legacy of faith, love, and strength.

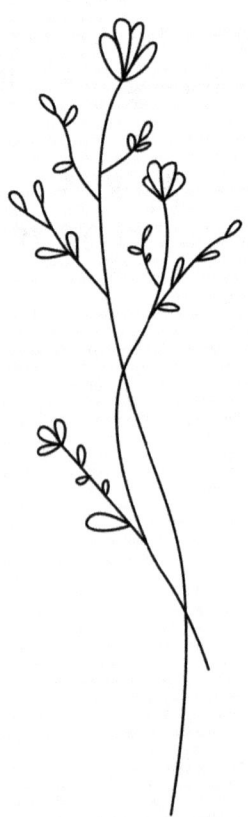

Table of Contents

INTRODUCTION

Planted In God's Word

It was in the month of April that God made a way for me to be home alone for three days. During those three days, I began to fast. My first day went well, and that night I dreamed of trees. They were big, beautiful, green trees with branches swaying back and forth in the wind. When I awoke, the thought of those trees lingered in my mind. I could not stop thinking about how they looked and how they moved in the breeze. Later that day, I searched online for the meaning of trees and found wisdom, creativity, and provision. I did not know what I expected to discover, but that answer surprised me. I sensed that my dream meant more than simply seeing trees.

After work, I went to the park for my usual run, listening to Bible verses and praying that God would reveal what He was trying to show me.

That weekend, I had lunch with a friend, and we talked for over four hours about church and family. Eventually, I shared my dream and explained how I felt God was trying to reveal something to me. She mentioned that her book study group was reading a book called *The Garden Within*. I almost cried because I knew again that God was speaking, even though I still did not fully understand His message.

The following Monday, after work, I changed clothes and went to the park, not to run this time, but simply to walk and be in God's presence. Out of habit, I began to run, but I quickly corrected myself, slowed down, and chose to walk instead. I took out my earbuds and listened to the sounds of nature.

As I walked, I noticed the trees surrounding the track and the park. I prayed that God would reveal the meaning of the trees. I saw how some were tall and strong while others were bent, short, or frail. Their trunks varied; some were thick and sturdy while others were slim and fragile. There were different kinds of trees—oak, maple, birch, and pine. I stopped at one tree, placed my hand on its trunk, and asked God what He was trying to tell me. That is when the Holy Spirit whispered, "Be planted in God's Word." Just like these trees were planted in the ground, I needed to be planted in God's Word. I repeated the phrase to myself over and over. That night, more things were revealed, but the most important truth remained: be planted in God's Word.

I searched the Scriptures and found many verses about trees, including:

- **Psalm 1:3 (NIV):** "That person is like a tree planted by streams of water, which yields its fruit in season and whose leaf does not wither—whatever they do prospers."
- **Mark 8:24 (NASB):** "He looked up and said, 'I see men; for I see them like trees walking.'"
- **Matthew 7:17 (ASV):** "Even so, every good tree produces good fruit, but the corrupt tree produces evil fruit."

Finding these Scriptures was enlightening and gave me a strong urge to do something with the message, "Be planted in God's Word." I asked myself if this was an idea for a T-shirt or something else. Then the Holy Spirit whispered, "Use this as a daily devotion." That is how this devotion was born.

I am not a writer, and I did not know the first thing about putting a book together, but God led me. There were times when I became busy and forgot about the book. Each time I got into my car, the Holy Spirit reminded me to finish it. At times, I would think to myself that I needed a new devotion, but the Holy Spirit reminded me that I already had one and needed to finish it. Sometimes I wondered how I would get the book published, but the Holy Spirit simply said, "Just finish, and I will do the rest."

How to Use This Devotional

There are 30 daily topics, each with a prayer journal, along with 6 prayer walk prompts. Put your phone away, find a quiet place and a time without distractions, and give God your full attention.

Every fifth day, you will find a Prayer Walk meditation. Use this time to walk and reflect on God's Word.

My prayer is that this devotional will be easy to understand and will help you on your journey to be planted in God's Word.

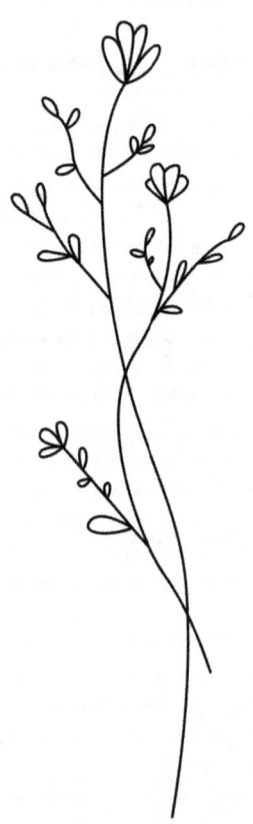

Day 1

Hope

But they who wait for the LORD shall renew
their strength; they shall mount up with wings
like eagles; they shall run and not be weary;
they shall walk and not faint.

Isaiah 40:31 (ESV)

What stands out to you when reading this scripture?

_____

_____

_____

_____

_____

_____

_____

_____

_____

_____

_____

_____

How can you apply this scripture to your life?

_____

_____

_____

_____

_____

_____

_____

_____

_____

_____

_____

_____

_____

_____

_____

_____

_____

_____

_____

_____

_____

_____

_____

_____

_____

What does "wait on God" look like for you?

_____

_____

_____

_____

_____

_____

_____

_____

_____

_____

_____

_____

_____

_____

_____

_____

_____

_____

_____

Daily Prayer Journal

Prayer Request

Praise Reports

Day 2

Comfort

Even though I walk through the valley of the shadow of death I will fear no evil for you are with me; your rod and your staff, they comfort me.

Psalm 23:4 (ESV)

What do you think the shadow of death means?

_____
_____
_____
_____
_____
_____
_____
_____
_____
_____
_____
_____
_____
_____

How does this passage help you face life's trials?

_____

_____

_____

_____

_____

_____

_____

_____

_____

_____

_____

_____

_____

_____

_____

_____

_____

_____

_____

_____

_____

_____

_____

_____

What promise is contained in this passage?

_____

_____

_____

_____

_____

_____

_____

_____

_____

_____

_____

_____

_____

_____

_____

_____

_____

_____

_____

_____

_____

_____

Daily Prayer Journal

Prayer Request

_____

_____

_____

_____

_____

_____

_____

_____

_____

_____

_____

_____

Praise Reports

_____

_____

_____

_____

_____

_____

_____

_____

Day 3

Be still

The LORD will fight for you, and you need only
to be still.

Exodus 14:14 (NIV)

What does this scripture mean to you?

_____

_____

_____

_____

_____

_____

_____

_____

_____

_____

_____

_____

_____

_____

_____

_____

How do you "be still" and allow God to fight for you?

_____

_____

_____

_____

_____

_____

_____

_____

_____

_____

_____

_____

_____

_____

_____

_____

_____

_____

_____

_____

_____

_____

❀ — ❀ — ❀ — ❀ — ❀

What are some things you need God to fight for you?

_____

_____

_____

_____

_____

_____

_____

_____

_____

_____

_____

_____

_____

_____

_____

_____

_____

_____

_____

_____

_____

_____

Daily Prayer Journal

Prayer Request

_____
_____
_____
_____
_____
_____
_____
_____
_____
_____
_____
_____
_____

Praise Reports

_____
_____
_____
_____
_____
_____
_____

Day 4

Forgiveness

Therefore, as God's chosen people, holy and dearly loved, clothe yourselves with compassion, kindness, humility, gentleness, and patience. Bear with each other and forgive one another if any of you has a grievance against someone. Forgive as the Lord forgave you.

Colossians 3:12–13 (NIV)

Why do you think forgiveness is important?

_____

_____

_____

_____

_____

_____

_____

_____

_____

_____

What makes forgiveness hard?

_____

_____

_____

_____

_____

_____

_____

_____

_____

_____

_____

_____

_____

_____

_____

_____

_____

_____

_____

_____

_____

_____

_____

❀ — ❀ — ❀ — ❀ — ❀

Is there someone you need to forgive? Who?
Explain?

_____

_____

_____

_____

_____

_____

_____

_____

_____

_____

_____

_____

_____

_____

_____

_____

_____

_____

_____

_____

_____

_____

_____

 **Daily Prayer Journal**

Prayer Request

_____
_____
_____
_____
_____
_____
_____
_____
_____
_____
_____
_____

Praise Reports

_____
_____
_____
_____
_____
_____
_____

Day 5

Prayer Walk

Pray this Scripture as you walk, and enjoy being in God's presence. Stay aware of your surroundings, and pray for whatever comes to your mind.

Psalm 23:1-3

The Lord is my shepherd; I shall not want. He makes me lie down in green pastures. He leads me beside still waters. He restores my soul" (ESV).

Reflect on God's guidance and restoration as you walk, trusting that He leads you in peace.

Daily Prayer Journal

Prayer Request

_____
_____
_____
_____
_____
_____
_____
_____
_____
_____
_____
_____
_____

Praise Reports

_____
_____
_____
_____
_____
_____
_____
_____

Day 6

Trust

But blessed is the one who trusts in the Lord whose confidence is in him. They will be like a tree planted by the water that sends out its roots by the stream. It does not fear when heat comes; leaves are always green. It has no worries in a year of drought and never fails to bear fruit.

Jeremiah 17:7-8 (NIV)

What does "They will be like a tree" mean to you?

_____
_____
_____
_____
_____
_____
_____
_____
_____
_____
_____

Why do we have a difficult time trusting in the Lord?

_____

_____

_____

_____

_____

_____

_____

_____

_____

_____

_____

_____

_____

_____

_____

_____

_____

_____

_____

_____

_____

_____

What does "Trust in the Lord" look like for you?

_____

_____

_____

_____

_____

_____

_____

_____

_____

_____

_____

_____

_____

_____

_____

_____

_____

_____

_____

_____

_____

_____

Daily Prayer Journal

Prayer Request

_____
_____
_____
_____
_____
_____
_____
_____
_____
_____
_____
_____
_____

Praise Reports

_____
_____
_____
_____
_____
_____
_____

Day 7

Tithing

Honor the Lord with your wealth and with the
first fruits of all your produce; then your barns
will be filled with plenty, and your vats will be
bursting with wine.

Proverbs 3:9-10 (ESV)

What stands out to you when reading this scripture?

_____

_____

_____

_____

_____

_____

_____

_____

_____

_____

_____

_____

_____

How do you honor the Lord with your wealth?

_____

_____

_____

_____

_____

_____

_____

_____

_____

_____

_____

_____

_____

_____

_____

_____

_____

_____

_____

_____

_____

What promise is contained in this scripture?

_____

_____

_____

_____

_____

_____

_____

_____

_____

_____

_____

_____

_____

_____

_____

_____

_____

_____

_____

_____

_____

_____

Daily Prayer Journal

Prayer Request

Praise Reports

Day 8

Faith

Faith is confidence in what we hope for and assurance about what we do not see.

Hebrews 11:1 (NIV)

How would you describe faith to others?

_____

_____

_____

_____

_____

_____

_____

_____

_____

_____

_____

_____

_____

_____

✿ — ✿ — ✿ — ✿ — ✿

What are some examples of how you show faith in God?

_____

_____

_____

_____

_____

_____

_____

_____

_____

_____

_____

_____

_____

_____

_____

_____

_____

_____

_____

_____

❀ — ❀ — ❀ — ❀ — ❀

Is faith something seen or done? Explain?

_____

_____

_____

_____

_____

_____

_____

_____

_____

_____

_____

_____

_____

_____

_____

_____

_____

_____

_____

_____

_____

_____

Daily Prayer Journal

Prayer Request

_____
_____
_____
_____
_____
_____
_____
_____
_____
_____
_____
_____
_____
_____

Praise Reports

_____
_____
_____
_____
_____
_____
_____
_____

Day 9

Fear

I sought the LORD, and he answered me; he
delivered me from all my fears.

Psalm 34:4 (NIV)

What makes you fearful?

_____

_____

_____

_____

_____

_____

_____

_____

_____

_____

_____

_____

_____

_____

_____

_____

Why do you think it is difficult to let go of our fears?

_____

_____

_____

_____

_____

_____

_____

_____

_____

_____

_____

_____

_____

_____

_____

_____

_____

_____

_____

_____

_____

_____

How do you handle fear biblically?

_____

_____

_____

_____

_____

_____

_____

_____

_____

_____

_____

_____

_____

_____

_____

_____

_____

_____

_____

_____

Daily Prayer Journal

Prayer Request

_____
_____
_____
_____
_____
_____
_____
_____
_____
_____
_____
_____

Praise Reports

_____
_____
_____
_____
_____
_____
_____

Day 10

Prayer Walk

Pray this scripture as you walk and enjoy being in God's presence. Be aware of your surroundings and pray for things as they come to your mind.

Psalm 119:105 (NIV)

"Your word is a lamp to my feet and a light to my path."

As you walk, this verse reminds you that God's Word guides you in both physical and spiritual journeys.

Daily Prayer Journal

Prayer Request

Praise Reports

Day 11

Wisdom

If any of you lack wisdom, you should ask God, who gives generously to all without finding fault, and it will be given to you.

James 1:5 (NIV)

What does this verse teach us about God's character?

_____

_____

_____

_____

_____

_____

_____

_____

_____

_____

_____

_____

_____

❀ — ❀ — ❀ — ❀ — ❀

How does having wisdom affect your personal growth?

_____

_____

_____

_____

_____

_____

_____

_____

_____

_____

_____

_____

_____

_____

_____

_____

_____

_____

_____

_____

_____

_____

◆

✿ — ✿ — ✿ — ✿ — ✿

How does having wisdom contribute to your overall decision-making?

_____

_____

_____

_____

_____

_____

_____

_____

_____

_____

_____

_____

_____

_____

_____

_____

_____

_____

_____

_____

Daily Prayer Journal

Prayer Request

_____

_____

_____

_____

_____

_____

_____

_____

_____

_____

_____

_____

Praise Reports

_____

_____

_____

_____

_____

_____

_____

Day 12

Obedience

But I gave them this command: Obey me, and
I will be your God and you will be my people.
Walk in obedience to all I command you,
that it may go well with you.

Jeremiah 7:23 (NIV)

How do you define obedience?

_____

_____

_____

_____

_____

_____

_____

_____

_____

_____

_____

_____

_____

According to this verse, what are the benefits of obedience?

_____

_____

_____

_____

_____

_____

_____

_____

_____

_____

_____

_____

_____

_____

_____

_____

_____

_____

_____

_____

_____

_____

Why do people struggle to obey God?

_____

_____

_____

_____

_____

_____

_____

_____

_____

_____

_____

_____

_____

_____

_____

_____

_____

_____

_____

_____

_____

Daily Prayer Journal

Prayer Request

Praise Reports

Day 13

God's Love

When you pass through the waters, I will be
with you; and when you pass through the
rivers, they will not sweep over you. When you
walk through the fire, you will not be burned;
the flames will not set you ablaze.

Isaiah 43:2 (NIV)

What are your thoughts on this verse?

_____

_____

_____

_____

_____

_____

_____

_____

_____

_____

_____

_____

❀ — ❀ — ❀ — ❀ — ❀

Can you describe any challenging experiences in your life that felt like navigating through deep water or enduring intense fires?

_____

_____

_____

_____

_____

_____

_____

_____

_____

_____

_____

_____

_____

_____

_____

_____

_____

_____

_____

✦

What is God telling us about his love for us?

_____

_____

_____

_____

_____

_____

_____

_____

_____

_____

_____

_____

_____

_____

_____

_____

_____

_____

_____

_____

_____

_____

Daily Prayer Journal

Prayer Request

_____
_____
_____
_____
_____
_____
_____
_____
_____
_____
_____
_____

Praise Reports

_____
_____
_____
_____
_____
_____
_____

Day 14

Grace

But he said to me, "My grace is sufficient for you, for my power is made perfect in weakness." Therefore, I will boast all the more gladly about my weaknesses, so that Christ's power may rest on me.

2 Corinthians 12:9 (NIV)

What does "My grace is sufficient" mean to you?

_____

_____

_____

_____

_____

_____

_____

_____

_____

_____

_____

_____

_____

Where in your life do you rely on God's grace to be sufficient?

_____

_____

_____

_____

_____

_____

_____

_____

_____

_____

_____

_____

_____

_____

_____

_____

_____

_____

_____

_____

_____

_____

_____

❀ — ❀ — ❀ — ❀ — ❀

What does "Christ's power is perfect in weakness" mean to you?

_____

_____

_____

_____

_____

_____

_____

_____

_____

_____

_____

_____

_____

_____

_____

_____

_____

_____

_____

Daily Prayer Journal

Prayer Request

_____

_____

_____

_____

_____

_____

_____

_____

_____

_____

_____

_____

Praise Reports

_____

_____

_____

_____

_____

_____

_____

Day 15

Prayer Walk

Pray this scripture as you walk and enjoy being in God's presence. Be aware of your surroundings and pray for things as they come to your mind.

Isaiah 40:31 (ESV)

But they who wait for the Lord shall renew their strength; they shall mount up with wings like eagles; they shall run and not be weary; they shall walk and not faint."

A powerful reminder of God's strength and renewal, especially when you might feel tired or worn.

Daily Prayer Journal

Prayer Request

Praise Reports

Day 16

Guidance

A man's heart plans his way, But the Lord
directs his steps

Proverbs 16:9 (NKJV)

**What does "A man's heart plans his way" mean to
you?**

_____

_____

_____

_____

_____

_____

_____

_____

_____

_____

_____

_____

_____

_____

❀ — ❀ — ❀ — ❀ — ❀

How does reading and studying the Bible help us comprehend God's guidance?

_____

_____

_____

_____

_____

_____

_____

_____

_____

_____

_____

_____

_____

_____

_____

_____

_____

_____

_____

_____

❀ — ❀ — ❀ — ❀ — ❀

Does having patience play a role in waiting on
God's guidance? Why?

_____

_____

_____

_____

_____

_____

_____

_____

_____

_____

_____

_____

_____

_____

_____

_____

_____

_____

_____

_____

_____

_____

Daily Prayer Journal

Prayer Request

_____

_____

_____

_____

_____

_____

_____

_____

_____

_____

_____

_____

Praise Reports

_____

_____

_____

_____

_____

_____

_____

Day 17

Gift / Talents

Each of you should use whatever gift you
have received to serve others, as faithful
stewards of God's grace in its various forms.

1 Peter 4:10 (NIV)

**Do you know what your spiritual gifts are? If so,
what are they?**

_____

_____

_____

_____

_____

_____

_____

_____

_____

_____

_____

_____

_____

❀ — ❀ — ❀ — ❀ — ❀

Do you think spiritual gifts are important? Why?

_____

_____

_____

_____

_____

_____

_____

_____

_____

_____

_____

_____

_____

_____

_____

_____

_____

_____

_____

_____

_____

_____

❀ — ❀ — ❀ — ❀ — ❀

How can you serve others with your spiritual gifts?

_____

_____

_____

_____

_____

_____

_____

_____

_____

_____

_____

_____

_____

_____

_____

_____

_____

_____

_____

_____

_____

✦

Daily Prayer Journal

Prayer Request

_____
_____
_____
_____
_____
_____
_____
_____
_____
_____
_____
_____

Praise Reports

_____
_____
_____
_____
_____
_____
_____

Day 18

Healing

Then they cried to the Lord in their trouble,
and He saved them from their distress. He sent
out his word and healed them; He rescued
them from the grave. Let them give thanks
to the Lord for His unfailing love and His
wonderful deeds for mankind.

Psalm 107:19-21 (NIV)

In what areas of your life have you felt distressed?

_____

_____

_____

_____

_____

_____

_____

_____

_____

_____

_____

What has God healed you from?

❀ — ❀ — ❀ — ❀ — ❀

What would you share with someone who is seeking healing?

_____

_____

_____

_____

_____

_____

_____

_____

_____

_____

_____

_____

_____

_____

_____

_____

_____

_____

_____

_____

_____

Daily Prayer Journal

Prayer Request

_____
_____
_____
_____
_____
_____
_____
_____
_____
_____
_____
_____
_____

Praise Reports

_____
_____
_____
_____
_____
_____
_____
_____

Day 19

Peace

Peace, I leave with you; my peace I give to
you. Not as the world gives do I give to you.
Let not your hearts be troubled, neither let
them be afraid.

John 14:27 (ESV)

How does the peace that Jesus offers compare to
the peace the world offers?

_____

_____

_____

_____

_____

_____

_____

_____

_____

_____

_____

❀ — ❀ — ❀ — ❀ — ❀

What does "don't let your heart be troubled" mean
to you?

_____

_____

_____

_____

_____

_____

_____

_____

_____

_____

_____

_____

_____

_____

_____

_____

_____

_____

_____

_____

_____

_____

✦

How does it feel to experience God's peace?

_____

_____

_____

_____

_____

_____

_____

_____

_____

_____

_____

_____

_____

_____

_____

_____

_____

_____

_____

Daily Prayer Journal

Prayer Request

_____

_____

_____

_____

_____

_____

_____

_____

_____

_____

_____

_____

_____

Praise Reports

_____

_____

_____

_____

_____

_____

_____

_____

Day 20

Prayer Walk

Pray this scripture as you walk and enjoy being in God's presence. Be aware of your surroundings and pray for things as they come to your mind.

Proverbs 3:5-6 (ESV)

"Trust in the Lord with all your heart, and do not lean on your own understanding. In all your ways acknowledge Him, and He will make straight your paths."

This encourages trust in God's guidance as you move forward in life.

Prayer Request

_____

_____

_____

_____

_____

_____

_____

_____

_____

_____

_____

_____

Praise Reports

_____

_____

_____

_____

_____

_____

_____

_____

Day 21

Perseverance

Consider it pure joy, my brothers, and sisters, whenever you face trials of many kinds, because you know that the testing of your faith produces perseverance. Let perseverance finish its work so that you may be mature and complete, not lacking anything.

James 1:2-4 (NIV)

How has your faith been tested?

_____

_____

_____

_____

_____

_____

_____

_____

_____

_____

❀ — ❀ — ❀ — ❀ — ❀

What does letting perseverance finish its work mean to you?

_____

_____

_____

_____

_____

_____

_____

_____

_____

_____

_____

_____

_____

_____

_____

_____

_____

_____

_____

_____

_____

How do you show perseverance?

_____

_____

_____

_____

_____

_____

_____

_____

_____

_____

_____

_____

_____

_____

_____

_____

_____

_____

_____

_____

_____

_____

Daily Prayer Journal

Prayer Request

_____
_____
_____
_____
_____
_____
_____
_____
_____
_____
_____
_____
_____

Praise Reports

_____
_____
_____
_____
_____
_____
_____
_____

Day 22

God's Protection

You are my hiding place; you will protect me from trouble and surround me with songs of deliverance.

Psalm 32:7 (NIV)

What does "My hiding place" mean to you?

_____

_____

_____

_____

_____

_____

_____

_____

_____

_____

_____

_____

_____

_____

_____

❀ — ❀ — ❀ — ❀ — ❀

How do you experience God's protection in your daily life?

_____

_____

_____

_____

_____

_____

_____

_____

_____

_____

_____

_____

_____

_____

_____

_____

_____

_____

_____

_____

_____

❀ — ❀ — ❀ — ❀ — ❀

What are the benefits of God's protection?

_____

_____

_____

_____

_____

_____

_____

_____

_____

_____

_____

_____

_____

_____

_____

_____

_____

_____

_____

_____

_____

_____

— ✦ —

Daily Prayer Journal

Prayer Request

Praise Reports

Day 23

Strength

So do not fear, for I am with you; do not be dismayed, for I am your God. I will strengthen you and help you; I will uphold you with my righteous right hand.

Isaiah 41:10 (NIV)

How can you draw on God's strength in difficult times?

_____

_____

_____

_____

_____

_____

_____

_____

_____

_____

_____

_____

Recall a time when you felt God strengthen you.

_____

_____

_____

_____

_____

_____

_____

_____

_____

_____

_____

_____

_____

_____

_____

_____

_____

_____

_____

_____

_____

_____

_____

❀ — ❀ — ❀ — ❀ — ❀

How can you rely on God to strengthen and help you?

_____

_____

_____

_____

_____

_____

_____

_____

_____

_____

_____

_____

_____

_____

_____

_____

_____

_____

_____

_____

_____

Daily Prayer Journal

Prayer Request

_____
_____
_____
_____
_____
_____
_____
_____
_____
_____
_____
_____
_____

Praise Reports

_____
_____
_____
_____
_____
_____
_____

Day 24

Temptation

No temptation has overtaken you except what is common to mankind. And God is faithful; he will not let you be tempted beyond what you can bear. But when you are tempted, he will also provide a way out so that you can endure it.

1 Corinthians 10:13 (NIV)

What are some causes of temptation in your daily life?

_____

_____

_____

_____

_____

_____

_____

_____

_____

_____

How do you know when you are being tempted?

_____

_____

_____

_____

_____

_____

_____

_____

_____

_____

_____

_____

_____

_____

_____

_____

_____

_____

_____

_____

_____

❀ — ❀ — ❀ — ❀ — ❀

List things you are tempted by. What are some ways
you can resist those temptations?

_____

_____

_____

_____

_____

_____

_____

_____

_____

_____

_____

_____

_____

_____

_____

_____

_____

_____

_____

_____

Daily Prayer Journal

Prayer Request

_____
_____
_____
_____
_____
_____
_____
_____
_____
_____
_____
_____
_____

Praise Reports

_____
_____
_____
_____
_____
_____
_____

Day 25

Prayer Walk

Pray this scripture as you walk and enjoy being in God's presence. Be aware of your surroundings and pray for things as they come to your mind.

Micah 6:8 (NIV)

He has shown you, O mortal, what is good. And what does the Lord require of you? To act justly and to love mercy and to walk humbly with your God."

A reminder to walk humbly and live justly with a heart of mercy.

Daily Prayer Journal

Prayer Request

Praise Reports

Day 26

Gods Will

Teach me to do your will, for you are my God!
Let your good Spirit lead me on level ground.

Psalm 143:10 (ESV)

Do you know God's will for your life? Explain?

_____

_____

_____

_____

_____

_____

_____

_____

_____

_____

_____

_____

_____

❀ — ❀ — ❀ — ❀ — ❀

How would you benefit from doing God's will?

_____

_____

_____

_____

_____

_____

_____

_____

_____

_____

_____

_____

_____

_____

_____

_____

_____

_____

_____

_____

_____

_____

_____

✦

❀ — ❀ — ❀ — ❀ — ❀

How can you support others in discovering and following God's will?

_____

_____

_____

_____

_____

_____

_____

_____

_____

_____

_____

_____

_____

_____

_____

_____

_____

_____

✦

Daily Prayer Journal

Prayer Request

_____
_____
_____
_____
_____
_____
_____
_____
_____
_____
_____
_____
_____

Praise Reports

_____
_____
_____
_____
_____
_____
_____
_____

Day 27

Worship

Whom have I in heaven but you?

And there is nothing on earth that I desire besides you.

Psalm 73:25 (ESV)

Why should you worship?

_____

_____

_____

_____

_____

_____

_____

_____

_____

_____

_____

_____

_____

_____

_____

❀ — ❀ — ❀ — ❀ — ❀

What is the purpose of worship for you?

_____
_____
_____
_____
_____
_____
_____
_____
_____
_____
_____
_____
_____
_____
_____
_____
_____
_____
_____
_____
_____
_____
_____
_____

❀ — ❀ — ❀ — ❀ — ❀

What are some reasons you worship God?

_____

_____

_____

_____

_____

_____

_____

_____

_____

_____

_____

_____

_____

_____

_____

_____

_____

_____

_____

_____

_____

_____

_____

_____

_____

Daily Prayer Journal

Prayer Request

Praise Reports

Day 28

Worry

Trust in the Lord with all your heart and lean not on your own understanding.

Proverbs 3:5 (NIV)

How can you apply this verse to your life?

_____

_____

_____

_____

_____

_____

_____

_____

_____

_____

_____

_____

_____

_____

What are some things you worry about?

❀ — ❀ — ❀ — ❀ — ❀

Why is it important to recognize that your thoughts may not always be accurate when you're feeling worried?

_____

_____

_____

_____

_____

_____

_____

_____

_____

_____

_____

_____

_____

_____

_____

_____

_____

_____

_____

_____

_____

◆

Daily Prayer Journal

Prayer Request

_____
_____
_____
_____
_____
_____
_____
_____
_____
_____
_____
_____
_____

Praise Reports

_____
_____
_____
_____
_____
_____
_____
_____

Day 29

Rejoicing

Rejoice in the Lord always; again, I will say, rejoice.

Philippians 4:4 (ESV)

What does it mean to (rejoice in the Lord?)

_____

_____

_____

_____

_____

_____

_____

_____

_____

_____

_____

_____

_____

_____

❀ — ❀ — ❀ — ❀ — ❀

Think about a difficult time in your life. How did you
stay focused and still rejoice in the Lord?

_____

_____

_____

_____

_____

_____

_____

_____

_____

_____

_____

_____

_____

_____

_____

_____

_____

_____

_____

_____

_____

_____

_____

_____

❀ — ❀ — ❀ — ❀ — ❀

What habits can you develop that will help you rejoice in the Lord each day?

_____

_____

_____

_____

_____

_____

_____

_____

_____

_____

_____

_____

_____

_____

_____

_____

_____

_____

_____

_____

Daily Prayer Journal

Prayer Request

_____

_____

_____

_____

_____

_____

_____

_____

_____

_____

_____

Praise Reports

_____

_____

_____

_____

_____

_____

_____

Day 30

Prayer Walk

Pray this scripture as you walk and enjoy being in God's presence. Be aware of your surroundings and pray for things as they come to your mind.

Deuteronomy 5:33 (NIV)

Walk in obedience to all that the Lord your God has commanded you, so that you may live and prosper and prolong your days in the land that you will possess."

A reminder to walk in the path of obedience and righteousness

Daily Prayer Journal

Prayer Request

_____
_____
_____
_____
_____
_____
_____
_____
_____
_____
_____
_____

Praise Reports

_____
_____
_____
_____
_____
_____
_____

Reflection

Reflect on how this devotion has influenced your personal life, behavior, and spiritual growth. Take note of any challenging topics that stretched you beyond your comfort zone. Set a goal or make a commitment to continue the spiritual habits you have developed over these 30 days.

_____

_____

_____

_____

_____

_____

_____

_____

_____

_____

_____

_____

_____

_____

_____

_____

_____

Closing Prayer

Lord, thank you for walking with me during this
30-day journey. I'm grateful for the wisdom
and clarity you've provided through your
word. Help me to continue growing in faith
and trust, and may these lessons stay rooted
in my heart as I navigate the days ahead.

Amen